Vocal Selections from the Off-Broadway Musical

T0087375

"HOUSE OF FLOWERS"

Lyrics by **TRUMAN CAPOTE** and **HAROLD ARLEN** Music by **HAROLD ARLEN**

AS RECORDED ON THE UNITED ARTISTS ORIGINAL CAST ALBUM

SIDE 1

	TITLE	ARTIST	PAGE
Band 1.	Preface: SMELLIN' OF VANILLA (Bamboo Cage)		
Band 2.	A SLEEPIN' BEE	Yolande Bavan, Thelma Oliver and Hope Clarke	2
Band 3.	SOMETHIN' COLD TO DRINK	Josephine Premice	6
Band 4.	HOUSE OF FLOWERS	Robert Jackson and Yolande Bavan	10
Band 5.	TWO LADIES IN DE SHADE OF DE BANANA TREE	Thelma Oliver and Hope Clarke	14
Band 6.	DON'T LIKE GOODBYES	Yolande Bavan	20
Band 7.	JUMP DE BROOM	Charles Moore & Company	24

SIDE 2

	TITLE	ARTIST	PAGE
Band 1.	SMELLIN' OF VANILLA (Bamboo Cage)	Thelma Oliver, Hope Clarke, Novella Nelson & Company	28
Band 2.	WAITIN'	Thelma Oliver and Hope Clarke	32
Band 3.	WIFE NEVER UNDERSTAN'	Robert Jackson	36
Band 4.	I NEVER HAS SEEN SNOW	Yolande Bavan	42
Band 5.	MADAME TANGO'S PARTICULAR TANGO	Novella Nelson, Carla Pinza, Hope Clarke and Thelma Oliver	48
Band 6.	WHAT IS A FRIEND FOR?	Tom Helmore and Josephine Premice	52
Band 7.	Duet Reprise: A SLEEPIN' BEE I NEVER HAS SEEN SNOW	Robert Jackson and Yolande Bavan	
Band 8.	Finale: TWO LADIES IN DE SHADE OF DE BANANA TREE	Josephine Premice, Hope Clarke, Thelma Oliver & Company	

©Copyright 1968 by Harold Arlen and Truman Capote
All rights throughout the world controlled by
HARWIN MUSIC CORPORATION, 810 Seventh Ave., New York, N.Y. 10019
International Copyright Secured   Made in U.S.A.   All Rights Reserved

44115

from the Off-Broadway Musical, "HOUSE OF FLOWERS"

A SLEEPIN' BEE

Lyric by
TRUMAN CAPOTE
and HAROLD ARLEN

Music by
HAROLD ARLEN

Very Moderately

Verse

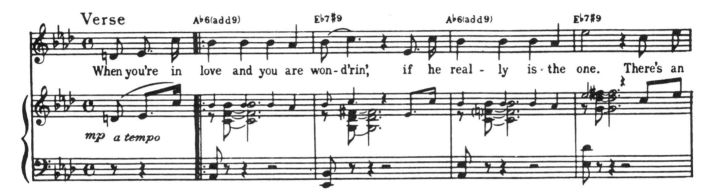

When you're in love and you are won-d'rin', if he real-ly is the one. There's an

an - cient sign sure to tell_ you if your search is o-ver and

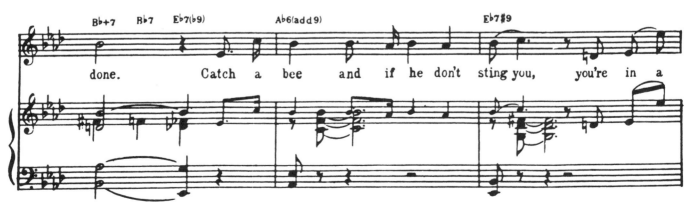

done. Catch a bee and if he don't sting you, you're in a

© Copyright 1954 by HAROLD ARLEN and TRUMAN CAPOTE
All rights throughout the world controlled by HARWIN MUSIC CORPORATION

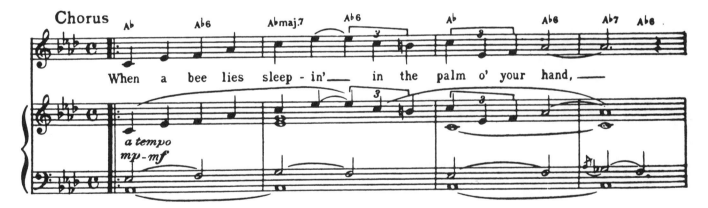

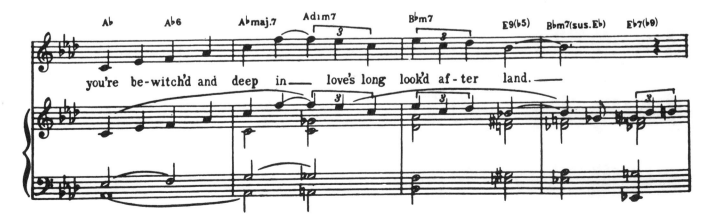

Where you'll see a sun-up sky with a morn-in' new, and

where the days go laugh-in' by as love comes a-call-in' on

you. Sleep on, Bee, don't wak-en,— can't be-lieve what just passed

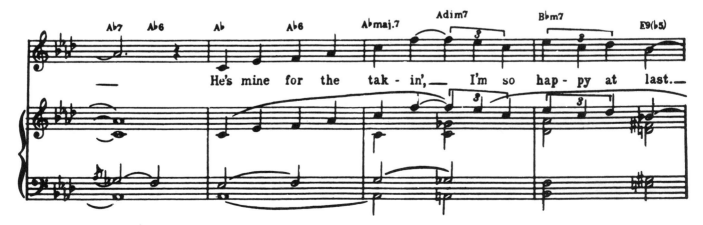

He's mine for the tak-in', I'm so hap-py at last.

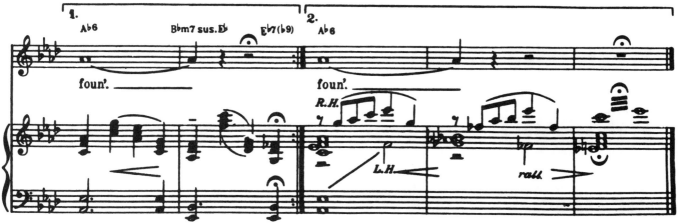

from the Off-Broadway Musical, "HOUSE OF FLOWERS"

SOMETHIN' COLD TO DRINK

Lyric by
**TRUMAN CAPOTE
and HAROLD ARLEN**

Music by
HAROLD ARLEN

© Copyright 1968 by HAROLD ARLEN and TRUMAN CAPOTE
All rights throughout the world controlled by HARWIN MUSIC CORPORATION

Refrain (*Not too fast - with vigor*)

SOME - THIN' COLD_ TO DRINK, de - light_ to taste, un - chaste
Some - thin' day_ by day each mat - i - nee O. K.

Some - thin' to_ ca - ress, an' ____ pos - sess un - dress.
Some - thin' naugh - ty nice, bring hand - some price, pre - cise.

Somethin' Cold etc. - 4

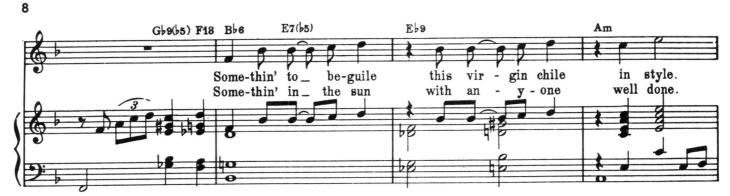

Somethin' to_ be-guile this vir-gin chile in style.
Somethin' in_ the sun with an-y-one well done.

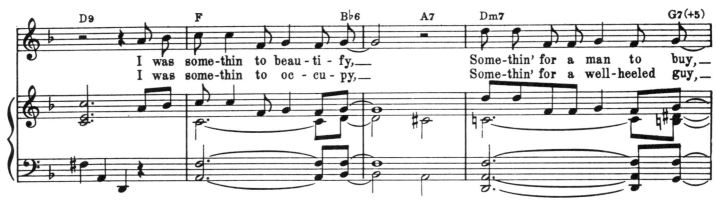

I was some-thin to beau-ti-fy,___ Some-thin' for a man to buy,___
I was some-thin to oc-cu-py,___ Some-thin' for a well-heeled guy,___

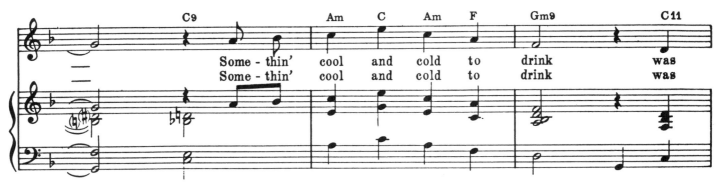

Some-thin' cool and cold to drink was
Some-thin' cool and cold to drink was

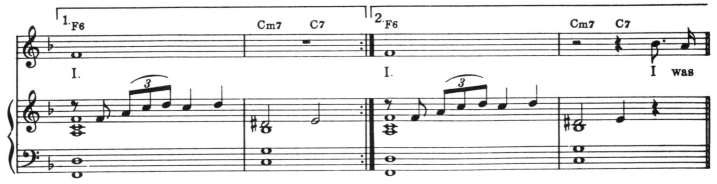

I.   I.
                                          I was

Interlude

jog-gled at, og-gled at, pre-paid an' gog-gled at, dan-died up, can-died up,

from the Off-Broadway Musical, "HOUSE OF FLOWERS"

HOUSE OF FLOWERS

Lyric by
TRUMAN CAPOTE
and HAROLD ARLEN

Music by
HAROLD ARLEN

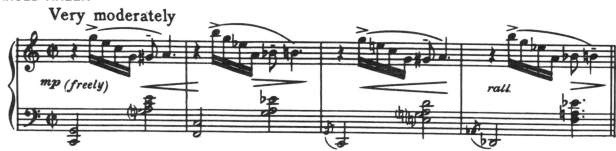

© Copyright 1954 by HAROLD ARLEN and TRUMAN CAPOTE
All rights throughout the world controlled by HARWIN MUSIC CORPORATION

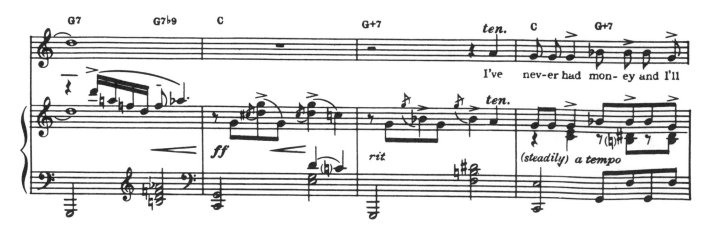

all those things___ what grows, what flies, what sings. If it all sounds temp-tin' and it

do you en-tice, I'd shout to the heav-en that it do make it nice. Won't you come

live with me?_ I'd come live with me,_ If I were you,_____ If I were you.____
(Ot-ti-lie)

My_____

JOSEPHINE PREMICE

from the Off-Broadway Musical, "HOUSE OF FLOWERS"

TWO LADIES IN DE SHADE OF DE BANANA TREE

Lyric by
TRUMAN CAPOTE
and **HAROLD ARLEN**

Music by
HAROLD ARLEN

© Copyright 1954 by HAROLD ARLEN and TRUMAN CAPOTE
All rights throughout the world controlled by HARWIN MUSIC CORPORATION

black, black shade of de Ba - na - na tree. _____ With lips
(Ba - nah - na)

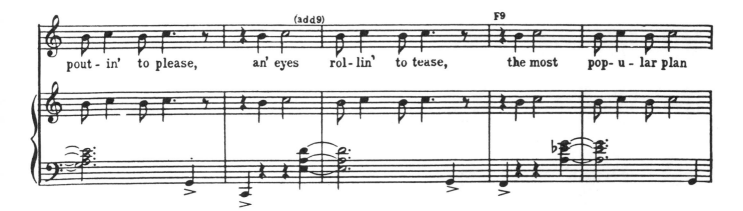

pout - in' to please, an' eyes rol - lin' to tease, the most pop - u - lar plan

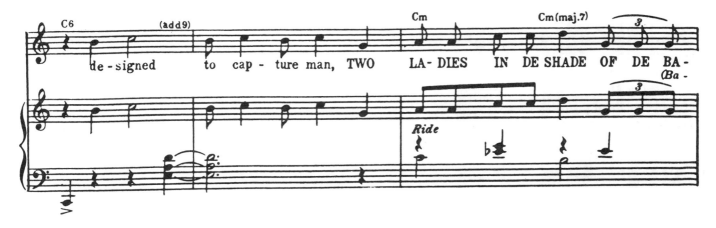

de - signed to cap - ture man, TWO LA - DIES IN DE SHADE OF DE BA -
(Ba -

NA - NA TREE. What a fro - lick - in spec - ta - cle they can be, _ In de
nah - na)

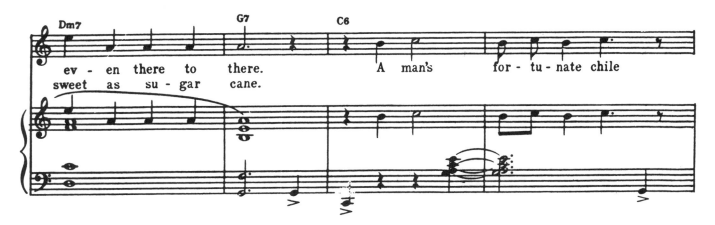

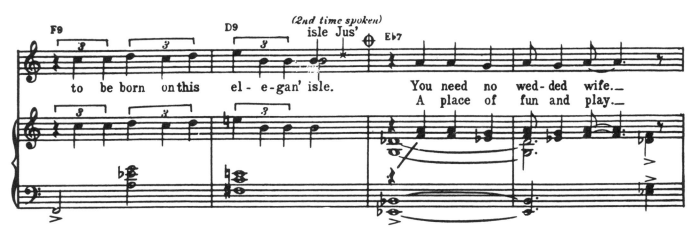

To taste the joys of life.___ Look? See? Nice? A-
Once here, you're here to stay.___

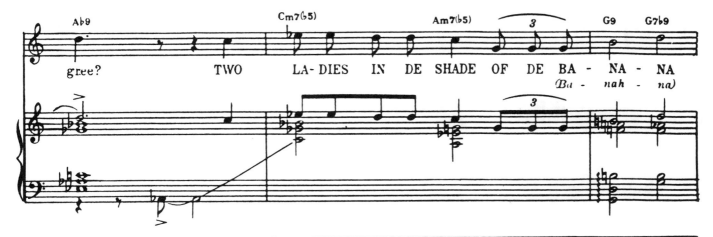

gree? TWO LA-DIES IN DE SHADE OF DE BA-NA-NA
(Ba - nah - na)

1.
TREE. ___

2.
laze a-way de day while de cock-a-too sings.

(Clap hands)

Fan-nin' yo face wid but-ter-fly wings. Shake to de mu-sic dat de

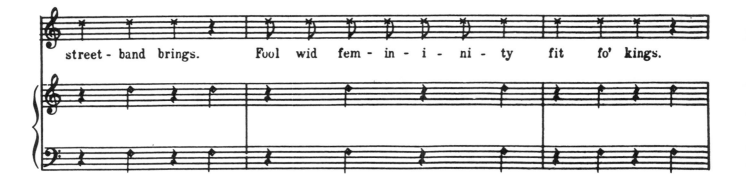

street - band brings. Fool wid fem - in - i - ni - ty fit fo' kings.

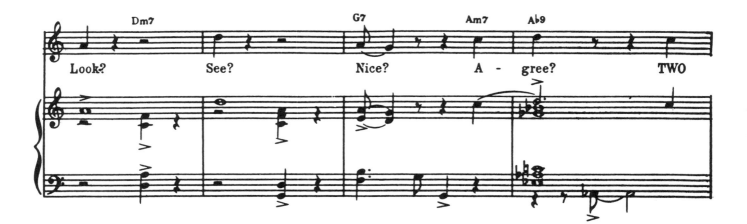

Look? See? Nice? A - gree? TWO

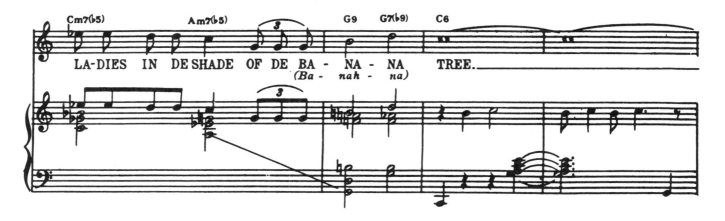

LA-DIES IN DE SHADE OF DE BA - NA - NA TREE.
(Ba - nah - na)

TOM HELMORE

from the Off-Broadway Musical, "HOUSE OF FLOWERS"

DON'T LIKE GOODBYES

Lyric by
TRUMAN CAPOTE
and HAROLD ARLEN

Music by
HAROLD ARLEN

DON'T LIKE GOOD-BYES, tears or sighs, I'm not too good at leav-in' time.

I got no taste for griev-in' time. No, no not me.

You've been my near one's, Al-ways my dear one's, I nev-er thought that

© Copyright 1954 by HAROLD ARLEN and TRUMAN CAPOTE
© Copyright 1963 by HAROLD ARLEN and TRUMAN CAPOTE
All rights throughout the world controlled by HARWIN MUSIC CORPORATION

Interlude

Have I found the an-swer?_ Yes. He's the on-ly an-swer._

molto rall. *a tempo*

Guess. I won't have to guide him,_ Jes,

molto rall. *a tempo* *molto rall.*

Walk be-side him, can't you see it clear-ly

slowly *rall.* *a tempo*

that I love him dear-ly._ Well, if you

D.S. 𝄋

from the Off-Broadway Musical, "HOUSE OF FLOWERS"

JUMP DE BROOM

Lyric by
TRUMAN CAPOTE

Music by
HAROLD ARLEN

Spirited

Everyone: JUMP DE BROOM de broom,

Ottilie jumps

Everyone: JUMP DE BROOM de broom,

Royal jumps JUMP DE BROOM de broom.

Cmaj7

Houngan: (1st time)
Everyone: (2nd time)

Cmaj7 Take de broom all a-roun', F9(♭5) Cmaj7 Sweep up de room, sweep up Dm7 (C) de groun'.

Intro to Royal-Ottilie dance

C6 C13(♭9)

Whistle: (Everyone)
(tacet)

(Percussion)

© Copyright 1967 by HAROLD ARLEN and TRUMAN CAPOTE
© Copyright 1968 by HAROLD ARLEN and TRUMAN CAPOTE
All rights throughout the world controlled by HARWIN MUSIC CORPORATION

Jump De Broom-4

Intro to Royal - Ottilie dance

Whistle: (Everyone)

After Dance Music

Houngan:

Time has come to JUMP DE BROOM, First de bride an' then de groom.

Dialogue___ Fleur and Jamison

Slowly -

Jump De Broom-4

from the Off-Broadway Musical, "HOUSE OF FLOWERS"

SMELLIN' OF VANILLA
(Bamboo Cage)

Lyric by
TRUMAN CAPOTE
and **HAROLD ARLEN**

Music by
HAROLD ARLEN

Moderately *(with a beat)*

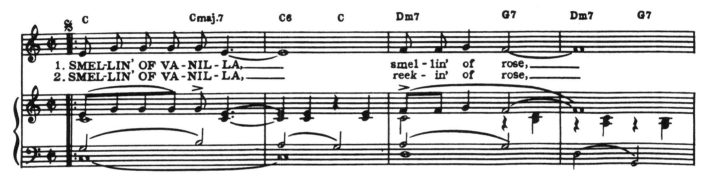

1. SMEL-LIN' OF VA-NIL-LA, smel-lin' of rose,
2. SMEL-LIN' OF VA-NIL-LA, reek-in' of rose,

decked 'n' dolled in our fin-est clothes. We're
decked 'n' dolled in our silk-en hose. We're

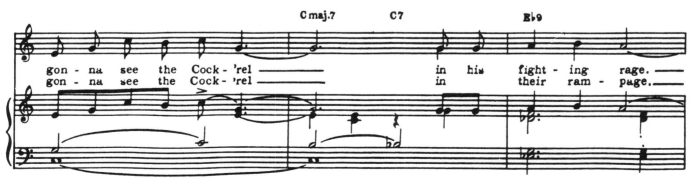

gon-na see the Cock-'rel in his fight-ing rage.
gon-na see the Cock-'rel in their ram-page.

© Copyright 1954 by HAROLD ARLEN and TRUMAN CAPOTE
© Copyright 1955 by HAROLD ARLEN and TRUMAN CAPOTE
All rights throughout the world controlled by HARWIN MUSIC CORPORATION

Make lit - tle o' de bird _____ in de Bam - boo Cage.
Make de feath-ers fly _____ out 'o de Bam - boo Cage.

Take Coda last time

Oh, de

Cock-'rel strut _____ by, wid a mean gleam in his eye. His

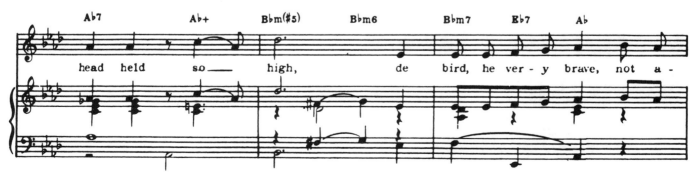

head held so _____ high, de bird, he ver - y brave, not a-

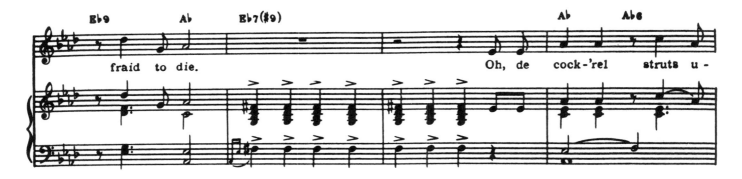

fraid to die.   Oh, de cock-'rel struts u-

nique,   as he sly - ly sharp-ens his beak,   proud-ly pro-me-nades his phys-

ique, de bird, he ver - y brave, cour-age   at   its peak.

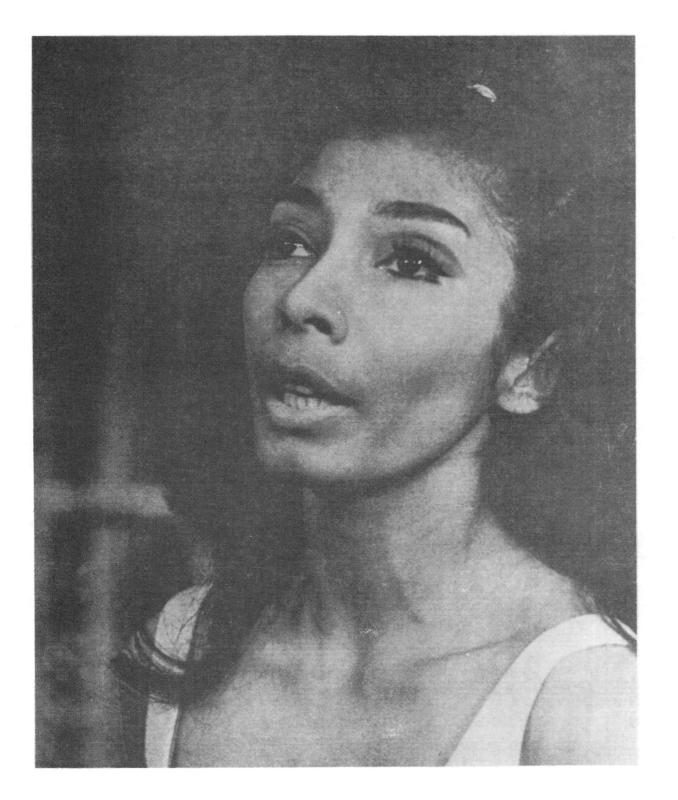

YOLANDE BAVAN

from the Off-Broadway Musical, "HOUSE OF FLOWERS"

WAITIN'

Lyric by
TRUMAN CAPOTE
and **HAROLD ARLEN**

Music by
HAROLD ARLEN

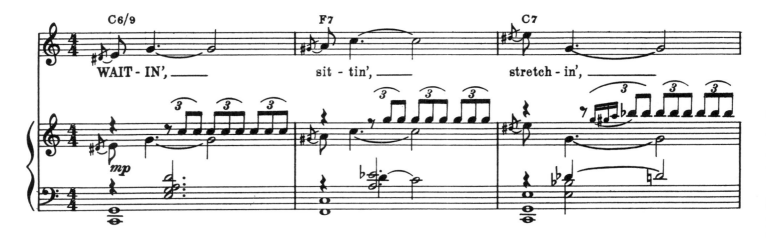

© Copyright 1954 by HAROLD ARLEN and TRUMAN CAPOTE
© Copyright 1968 by HAROLD ARLEN and TRUMAN CAPOTE
All rights throughout the world controlled by HARWIN MUSIC CORPORATION

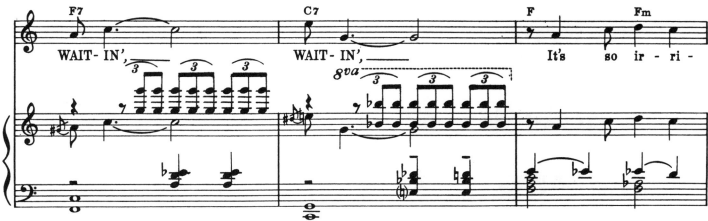

Waitin' - 8

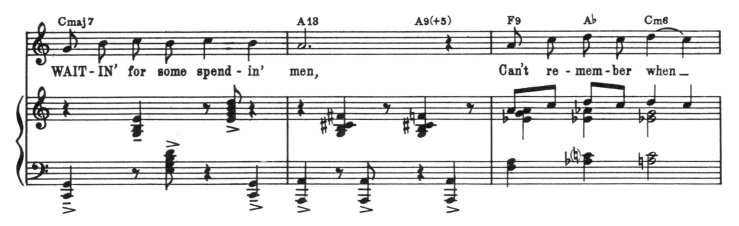

WAIT - IN' for some spend - in' men, Can't re - mem - ber when __

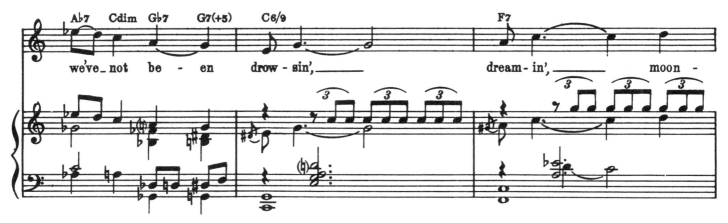

we've __ not be - en drow - sin', _____ dream - in', _____ moon -

beam - in' _____ 'bout the thing __ we're su - preme in, _____ And

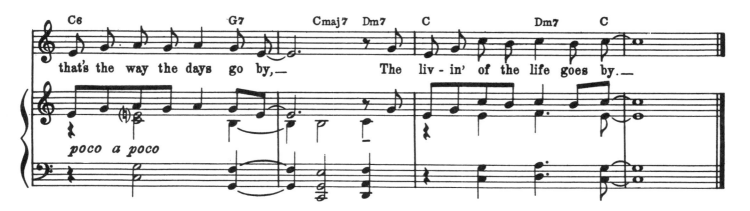

that's the way the days go by, __ The liv - in' of the life goes by. __

poco a poco

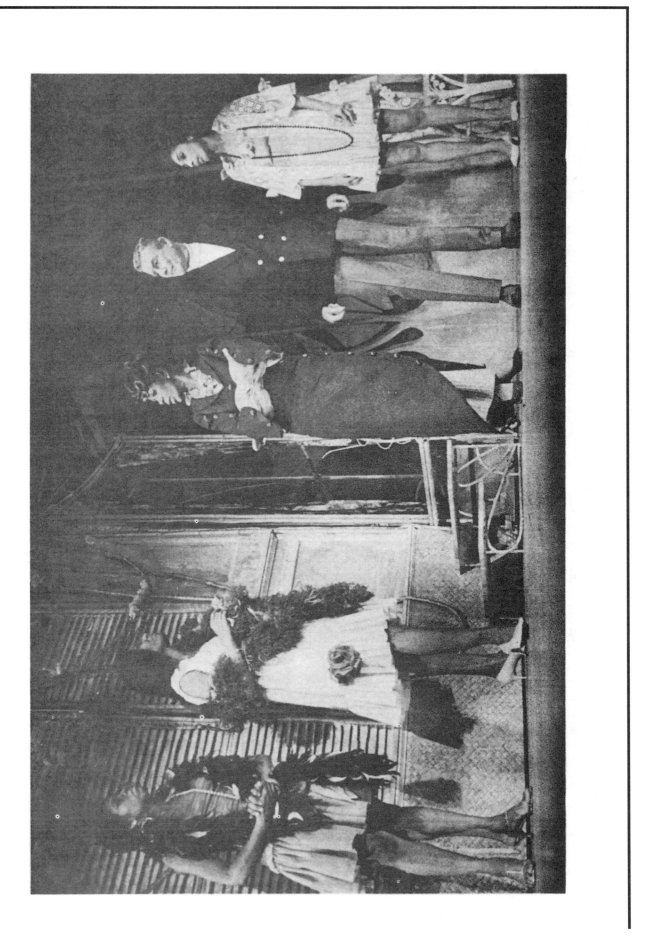

from the Off-Broadway Musical, "HOUSE OF FLOWERS"

WIFE NEVER UNDERSTAN'

Lyric by
TRUMAN CAPOTE
and **HAROLD ARLEN**

Music by
HAROLD ARLEN

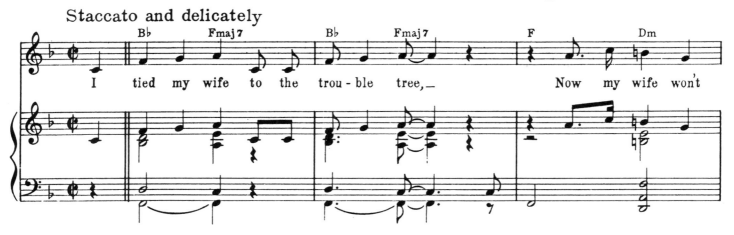

© Copyright 1967 by HAROLD ARLEN and TRUMAN CAPOTE
© Copyright 1968 by HAROLD ARLEN and TRUMAN CAPOTE
All rights throughout the world controlled by HARWIN MUSIC CORPORATION

Husban' doin' what he can.___

I tied my wife to the tri - bal tree,___ Now she act so

fool - ish - ly;___ She say she fly a - way a - ban - don - ing me,

'Cause de lit - tle wom - an she tied to the tri - bal tree.

Oh, Ot - til - ie, look at_ me, How come_ you so an - gry?

Good-ness hon - ey, don't you see,_ I on - ly do-in' my du - ty._

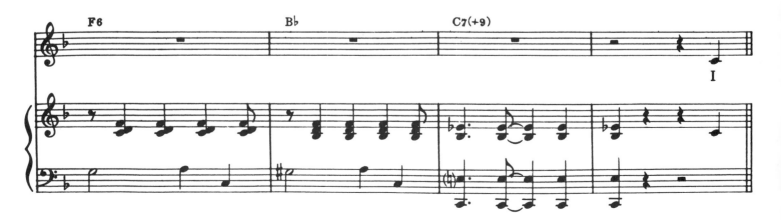

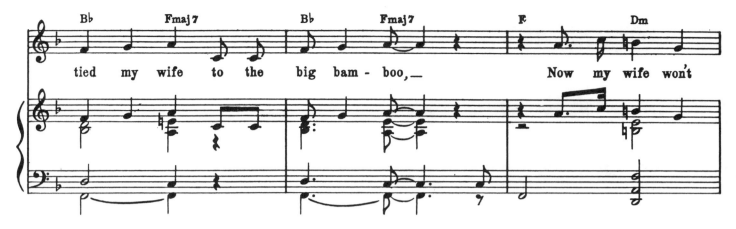

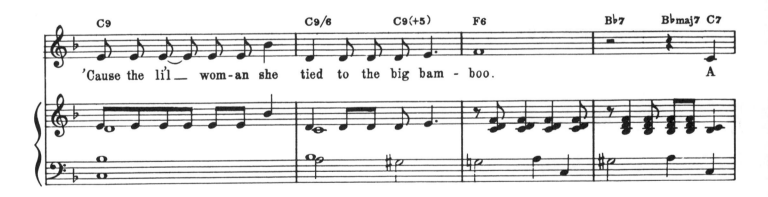

Woman Never Understan' - 5

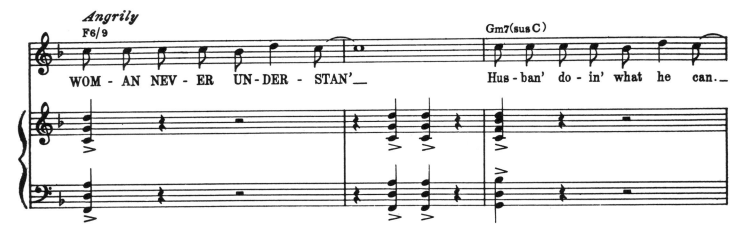

from the Off-Broadway Musical, "HOUSE OF FLOWERS"

I NEVER HAS SEEN SNOW

Lyric by
TRUMAN CAPOTE
and HAROLD ARLEN

Music by
HAROLD ARLEN

© Copyright 1954 by HAROLD ARLEN and TRUMAN CAPOTE
All rights throughout the world controlled by HARWIN MUSIC CORPORATION

closed the door on the girl
boy I was be-fore.

Slow, but steady

Feel-in' fine and full o' bliss, what I real-ly wants to say is

this:

Chorus

I NEV-ER HAS SEEN SNOW, all the same I know,

Snow ain't so beau-ti-ful,___ C'ain't be so beau-ti-ful like my

love is, Like my love is.

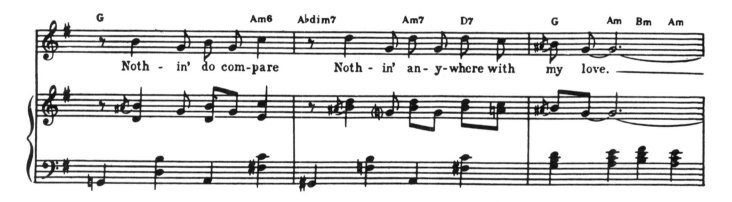

Noth - in' do com-pare Noth - in' an - y-where with my love. ___

A hun- dred things I see_____ A

twi-light sky, that tree,_____ but none so beau-ti-ful,_____

not one so beau-ti-ful, like my love is, like my love is.

molto rall. *a tempo* *ten.*

Once you see his face, none can take the place of

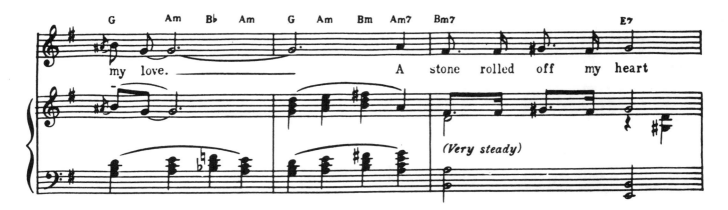

my love._____ A stone rolled off my heart

(Very steady)

When I laid my eyes on that near to me boy/gal with that far a-way look,— and

right from the start,— I saw a new hor - i - zon and a

road to take me where I want - ed to be took,

need - ed to be took,— and

though _____ I NEV - ER HAS SEEN SNOW.

All the same I know noth-in' will ev-er be, noth-in can ev-er be

beau - ti - ful as my love is, like my love is to me. _____

I

from the Off-Broadway Musical, "HOUSE OF FLOWERS"

MADAME TANGO'S PARTICULAR TANGO

Lyric by
TRUMAN CAPOTE
and **HAROLD ARLEN**

Music by
HAROLD ARLEN

© Copyright 1967 by HAROLD ARLEN and TRUMAN CAPOTE
© Copyright 1968 by HAROLD ARLEN and TRUMAN CAPOTE
All rights throughout the world controlled by HARWIN MUSIC CORPORATION

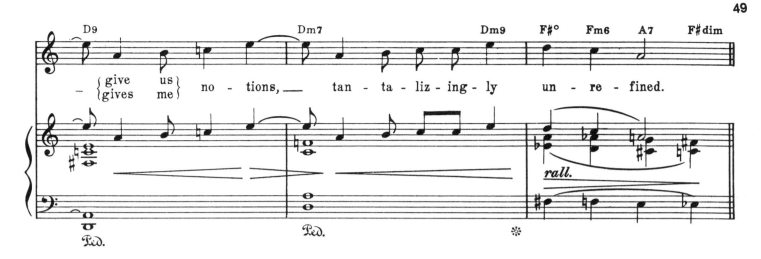

Chords: D9, Dm7, Dm9, F#°, Fm6, A7, F#dim

{give us}
{gives me} no - tions, ___ tan - ta - liz - ing - ly un - re - fined.

rall.

Ped. *Ped.* ✳

Tacet

a tempo *mf*

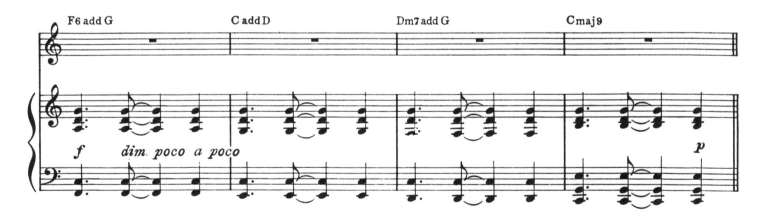

Chords: F6 add G, C add D, Dm7 add G, Cmaj9

f *dim. poco a poco* *p*

Refrain

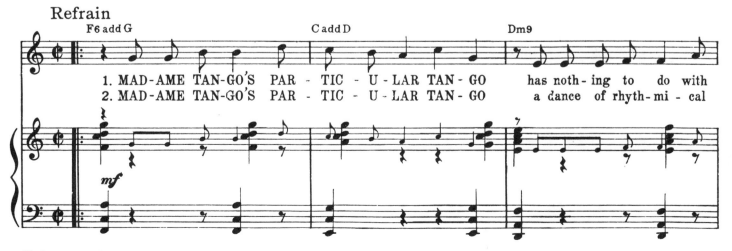

Chords: F6 add G, C add D, Dm9

1. MAD-AME TAN-GO'S PAR - TIC - U - LAR TAN - GO has noth-ing to do with
2. MAD-AME TAN-GO'S PAR - TIC - U - LAR TAN - GO a dance of rhyth-mi - cal

mf

Madame etc.-4

things ce - les - tial,   MAD-AME TAN-GO'S PAR - TIC - U - LAR TAN - GO
com - po - si - tion.   MAD-AME TAN-GO'S PAR - TIC - U - LAR TAN - GO

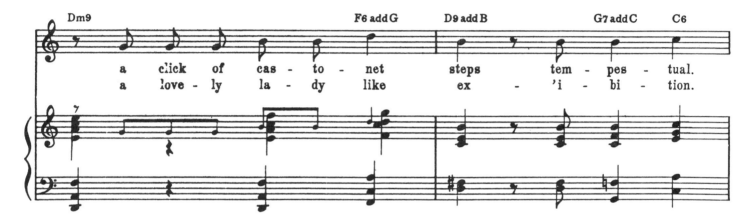

a click of cas - to - net   steps   tem - pes - tual.
a love - ly la - dy like   ex - 'i - bi - tion.

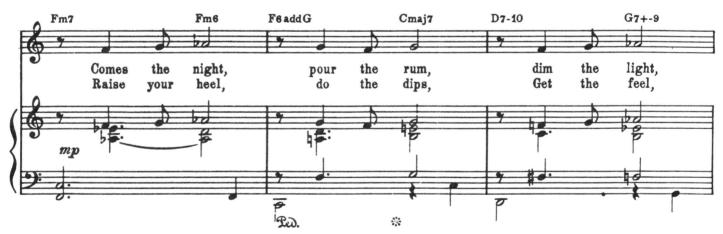

Comes the night,   pour the rum,   dim the light,
Raise your heel,   do the dips,   Get the feel,

tap the drum;   Flip your hips,   sug - ar plum, then
flip your hips;   Tres gen - teel   fin - ger tips then

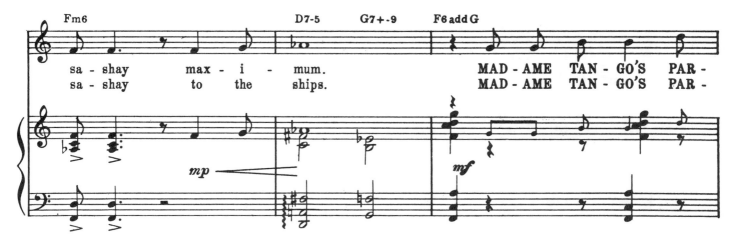

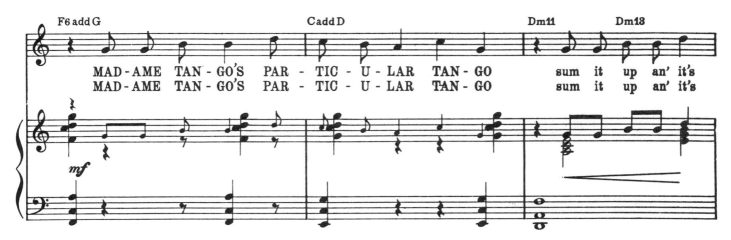

Madame etc.- 4

from the Off- Broadway Musical, "HOUSE OF FLOWERS"

WHAT IS A FRIEND FOR?

Lyric by
TRUMAN CAPOTE
and **HAROLD ARLEN**

Music by
HAROLD ARLEN

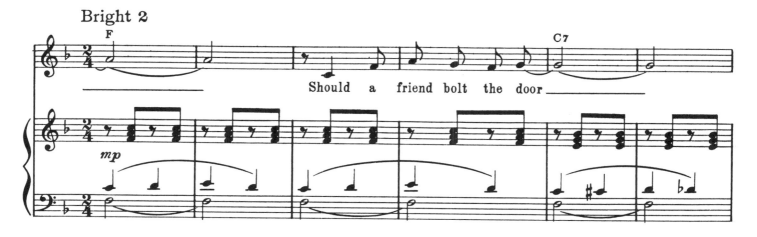

© Copyright 1967 by HAROLD ARLEN and TRUMAN CAPOTE
© Copyright 1968 by HAROLD ARLEN and TRUMAN CAPOTE
All rights throughout the world controlled by HARWIN MUSIC CORPORATION

met - a - phor for good times and noth - ing more?

(tacet) A friend-ship's nev - er com - plete_____ On a

one - way street,_____ Takes the two - way test_

_ to bring_ out_ the best, All the rest is just sheer bad - i - nage,

What's A etc. -9

On - ly a mere mi - rage.___ Who needs a

Moderate 4

friend with a hast - y heart___ who's on - ly pleased with the tast - y

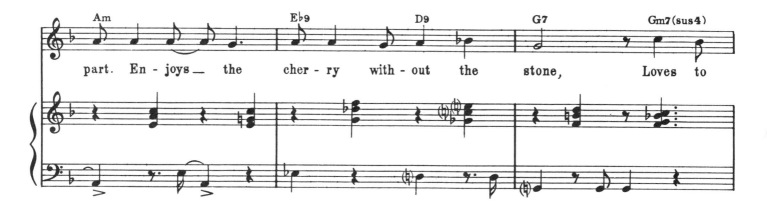

part. En - joys___ the cher - ry with - out the stone, Loves to

love but live a - lone.___ To my mind there's noth - in'

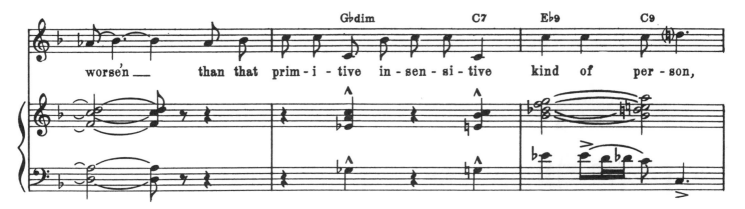

worse'n ___ than that prim - i - tive in - sen - si - tive kind of per - son,

Bright 2

(tacet)

I like a friend to be, _____ A

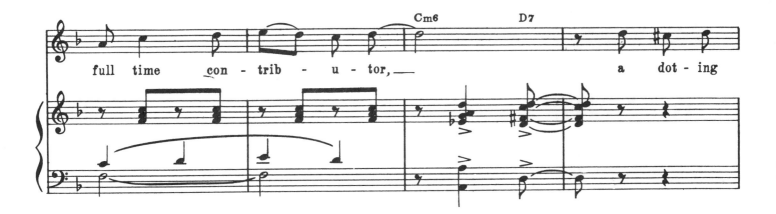

full time con - trib - u - tor, ___ a dot - ing

dev - o - tee. ___ That's what an all out friend ___ is

What's A etc. - 9

for.

I like my dai-quir-is strong,—

Bright 4

I like my lov-in' long,— If my heart you would move,

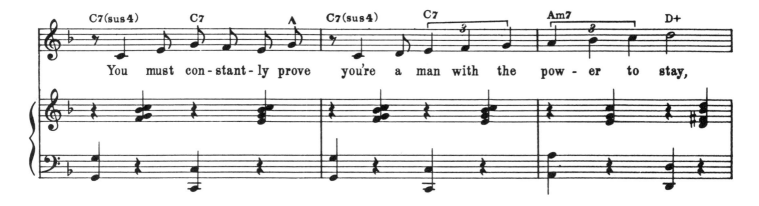

You must con-stant-ly prove you're a man with the pow - er to stay,

Real men don't fade a - way, Give me my talk-in' straight,—

What's A etc.-9

night, then leaves you to your-self. In my mind I

draw the line_____ At that kind of e - go - tis - ti - cal,

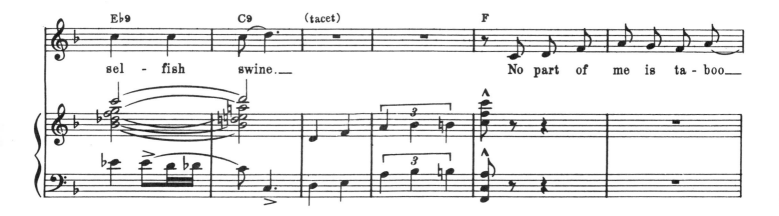

sel - fish swine.___ No part of me is ta-boo___

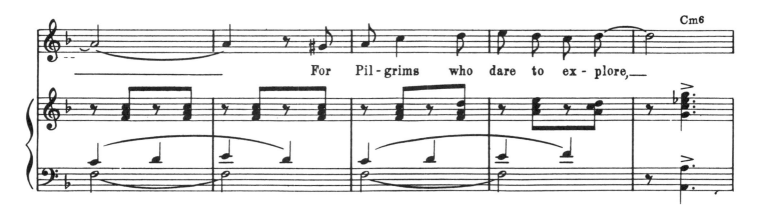

For Pil - grims who dare to ex - plore,___

One who will fol-low through,___ that's what a full time friend___

Moderate 4

___ is for._____ You're not sleep-in' well,

Life's an emp-ty shell, Breath-in' seems a chore,

Bright 2

What you need to do is to find your-self a friend

What's A etc.-9

who might ex - plore. Then mod - u - late

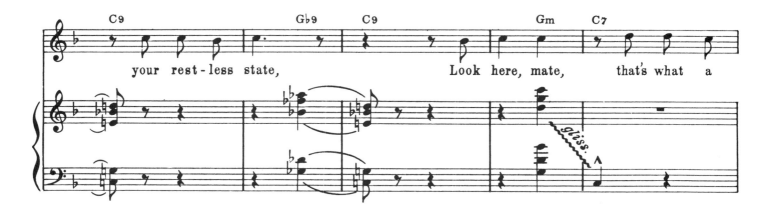

your rest - less state, Look here, mate, that's what a

friend is for.

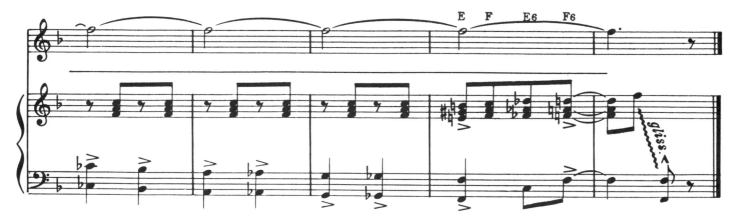

HAROLD ARLEN

and TRUMAN CAPOTE